EXTREME FIGHTERS

BLACKBIRCH PRESS

An imprint of Thomson Gale, a part of The Thomson Corporation

THOMSON

★

GALE

Detroit • New York • San Francisco • San Diego • New Haven, Conn. • Waterville, Maine • London • Munich

LIBRARY OF CONGRESS CATALOGING-IN-PUBLICATION DATA

Fighters / John Woodward, book editor
  p. cm. — (Planet's most extreme)

Includes bibliographical references and index.
  ISBN: 1-4103-0383-7 (hard cover : alk. paper)
    1-4103-0412-4 (paper cover : alk. paper)
  1. Animal behavior—Juvenile literature. 2. Risk-taking (Psychology) — Juvenile litera-ture. I. Woodward, John, 1958- II. Title III. Series.

Printed in the United States of America
10 9 8 7 6 5 4 3 2 1

Are you ready to rumble? Well, stand by for action, because we're going head to head with the best warriors in the natural world. We're counting down the top ten most extreme fighters in the animal kingdom and seeing how they stack up against human attempts to battle their way into the record books. Discover that all's fair in love and war when fighting is taken to The Most Extreme.

10

The Lion

Take a close look at the cat. For inside this hunter is the heart of an animal that's roaring into number ten in the countdown! The lion is king of the jungle, but only because it knows how to fight for its kingdom.

**Roaring into number ten, the king
of the jungle is a fearsome fighter.**

The lion is built to fight. It can weigh more than three
men, and has enough muscle to break a zebra's back
with a single blow. It's number ten in the countdown
because for thousands of years, lions were a worthy
foe for the strongest fighters in history.

The male lion that proves himself as the best fighter gets all the girls!

All animals have to fight for food, or shelter, or a mate. And in the animal kingdom it's the best fighter that usually gets the girl.

The male lion that's the best fighter has all the girls too. But since all he has to do is fight off other males, he has lots of time to do what males do best.

Lions are only number ten in the countdown because although they're great fighters, they can sleep up to 20 hours each day! It's the females who have to do all the hard work of hunting and raising the kids.

A lioness is a fighter in her own right, though. In fact, sometimes lazy males can get a lesson about the strength of girl power. Perhaps we should be calling the lion the "queen of the jungle."

Lions are great fighters, but they're even better sleepers.

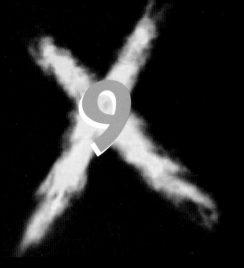

The
Bombardier Beetle

At number nine in the countdown is a truly extreme fighting machine, with armor plating outside and high explosive inside. It's found in battlefields around the world. You just have to know where to look.

The bombardier beetle has a built-in bomb.

Blasting its way into number nine in the countdown is a bug with a bomb in its bottom. The bombardier beetle gets its name because it blasts boiling hot toxic chemicals out its backside. But the beetle has a challenge. How do you make sure the bomb doesn't blow your bottom off? The secret lies in keeping the two explosive ingredients well separated. In one gland it stores hydrogen peroxide—a potent chemical humans use as rocket fuel.

This beetle has a gland full of hydrogen peroxide.

The beetle squirts a little into a reaction chamber and then adds enzymes. The result is explosive! The beetle can fire its cannon 700 times a second! This same kind of explosion was created in a very different kind of bug. The "doodlebug" was the nick-name of the V-1 rocket manufactured by Germany in World War II. These flying bombs were powered by an engine that bore an uncanny resemblance to the bombardier beetle's backside. The pulsing series of explosions gave the V-1 rockets several nicknames. As well as "doodlebugs," they were called "buzz bombs!"

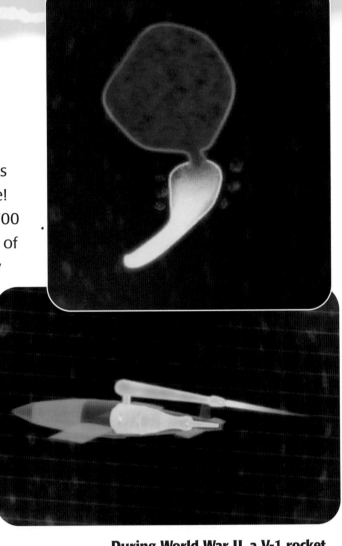

During World War II, a V-1 rocket (bottom) used the same technique as the beetle (top) and even got its nickname from the "doodlebug."

This spider thinks it has a meal in the bag, but it messed with the wrong beetle.

The bombardier beetle packs a punch in its pants— not to fly, but to fight. Thanks to this secret weapon, the spider ends up with a burnt face full of toxic chemicals, while the beetle lives to fight an other day.

8

The **Elephant Seal**

Some fighters have a nose for trouble. The elephant seal gets its name not only from that trunklike snout, but because it is very, very big. It's as large as a Volkswagen and twice as heavy.

Elephant seals have a lot of weight to throw around.

When it comes to throwing weight around, nothing can compare with elephant seals. The bigger they are, the better their chances of mating. A bull fights to control the beach, because on the beach is his harem. Up to fifty females can be jealously guarded by a single male.

A bull seal has to fight off other males to keep control of his harem.

But it's not easy looking after all those females. The harem is an attractive target for all the other males. They don't get a chance to mate unless they can beat the beach master.

As well as being incredibly fat, bull elephant seals have developed a thick calloused chest shield as protection against all the pushing and shoving. And in Japan, some humans have done much the same thing.

There's no weight class in sumo wrestling, so in this sport as with elephant seals, bigger is usually better. Wrestlers also have a secret weapon. Their loincloths are never washed. The wrestlers believe if you wash the loincloth, you might wash away all the wrestler's experience. Considering that a professional sumo wrestler's career can last more than ten years, there's an awful lot of experience in that loincloth! Bull elephant seals need both great experience and great size to keep control of their harem. But sometimes, the biggest bulls on the beach don't always get the girl.

This sneaky bull is getting the last laugh. He's found an unguarded female.

A sneaky male will wait for the beach master to have his hands full with the latest challenger. Then he makes his move. It's a race to find an unguarded female before the beach master realizes there's an intruder in the harem! It just goes to show that sometimes brains really are better than brawn.

7 The **Praying Mantis**

We're lucky the praying mantis only grows to enormous size in horror movies, because this really is one bad bug. It's number seven in the countdown because this fighter strikes with lightning speed.

The spectral tarsier is a hundred times heavier than its prey.

But the mantis has the moves!

So when it comes to fighting, just how good is a mantis? Catching harmless insects is one thing. But it can also take on a spectral tarsier! This Indonesian primate is a hundred times heavier than a mantis, and hunts bugs for a living.

If a mantis can fight off a hungry hunter like the tarsier, it's not surprising that some humans have tried to copy its moves. Welcome to kung fu . . . mantis style. About 400 years ago, a Chinese martial arts master called Wong Long was really impressed by the praying mantis's concentration and devastatingly fast strike.

Praying Mantis Kung Fu enables people to take down bigger and stronger opponents . . . just like the mantis does!

Today variations of Praying Mantis Kung Fu are practiced all over the world, including here in Honolulu, with instructor Sifu David Moragne. He explains:

> We imitate the insect. It makes the kung fu kind of sneaky and very powerful. People go "Oh, what happened?" or "How did that happen?" Nobody knows—you're not broadcasting, you're not telling anyone what you're about to do.

> Once you make contact, you know automatically that at the top of the arm is the head, so you don't have to think about it. You can just strike.

> You use the other person's energy against them. So if a person's pushing against you, you don't have to resist. There's always someone stronger than you, so why play the game of trying t o match someone's strength?

Unfortunately, the strength of the mantis causes problems when it's time to play a different kind of game. Because the female mantis is such a lethal fighter, the smaller male really puts his body on the line when it's time to mate. Sometimes things go horribly wrong. The female may bite off the male's head.

Fortunately, the male can continue mating without its head. It's not much fun for the male, but at least the female gets a good dose of protein, which will provide a head start for her eggs and the next generation of extreme fighters.

Mating is a dangerous game for the much smaller male mantis.

The Polar Bear

To find number six in the countdown, you have to travel to the frozen wastes of the Arctic. The polar bear doesn't have many friends. It's a solitary animal, and likes it that way. For when two bears are after the same food or mate, bad things happen.

Only one animal could win a fight with a polar bear . . . another polar bear!

Polar bears are number six in the countdown because they are devastating fighters. An adult bear can weigh as much as seven men. One swipe of its huge paw could take out prey three times its size.

There's really only one animal that could take on a polar bear and win, and that's another polar bear. They're just too big and too fast. So it's no wonder the bear was an inspiration for a group of human warriors.

Some Viking warriors believed that bearskin shirts gave them the power to fight like real bears.

A thousand years ago, Europe was terrorized by the Vikings. And the most feared Vikings of all were those fighters who believed that if they wore a specially treated bearskin shirt (called a bear-sark), something amazing would happen. The warrior would magically gain the fighting abilities of the bear!

In their magic bearskins, the warriors went totally nuts. They fought in such a frenzy that it was from the Viking's "bear-sark" that we got the word *berserk.*

The terrible fighting abilities of the bear still fascinate people today. But luckily for the polar bear, now when people go berserk, they don't need a bearskin shirt.

These adult polar bears can weigh as much as seven men.

The **Musk Oxen**

One animal knows that when it comes to fighting, it pays to use your head. This is a musk ox. It's number five in our countdown because underneath that shaggy coat is the most extreme head-banger on the planet.

Musk oxen are pretty peaceful, until two males come head to head.

Most of the time, musk oxen graze peacefully on the Arctic tundra. But when two males get together, it's best to get out of the way.

Males run at 20 miles an hour when they charge.

This tooth-rattling collision would kill a human, yet males will charge at each other up to 20 times or more during a fight. Hurtling towards each other at 20 miles an hour would be like going headfirst into a car wreck!

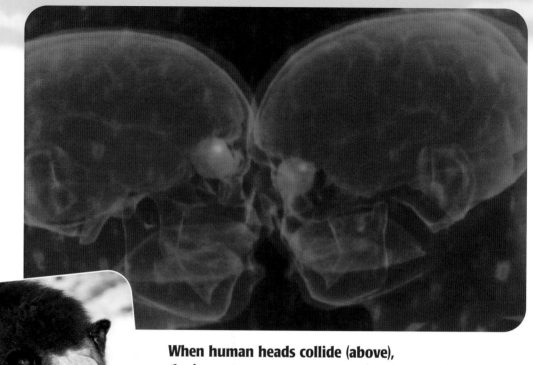

When human heads collide (above), the impact can cause a concussion, but musk oxen have much more bone to protect their brains.

Musk oxen survive their head-on crashes because they're the biggest boneheads on the planet. There are 4 inches of horn and 3 inches of bone directly over the brain in the area of impact. Humans don't have this cushioning, which.can be a problem on a different kind of field.

Today, only a special breed of warrior charges headfirst into the opposition. Football players can collide at 15 miles per hour. The trouble is that in the collision, the brain keeps moving when the skull stops. When the brain crashes into the skull, we get a concussion because the impact damages the delicate nerve tissue. That's why we invented the helmet. By absorbing the shock of impact, it helps protect the brain.

The most extreme helmets were worn by medieval knights who fought like the musk ox. Protection came not from 4 inches of bone in the skull, but from elaborate suits of armor that weighed half as much as the knight! You needed all the protection you could get when you sat on top of a half a ton of warhorse charging at 25 miles an hour.

Even with suits of armor, knights were killed or maimed at jousting tour-naments. People needed to find a new way of fighting with lances, which is how we ended up with a toy that's still in use today! The carousel was originally developed with dummies riding on the toy horses, which were much safer targets for a charging knight.

Medieval knights fought like musk oxen when they jousted, but they wore heavy armor for protection.

4

The Madagascan
Ring-tailed Lemur

Jousting may be child's play for the musk ox, but when our next contender fights, it's a family affair! Sliding in at number four is the most unusual fighter in the countdown.

They may look cute and cuddly, but these Madagascan ring-tailed lemurs are fearsome fighters.

Here at Orana Park in New Zealand, people have had to build a moat to keep this contender contained. For while this animal can't swim—it can fight. At number four in the countdown is the Madagascan ring-tailed lemur—the cuddliest animal in the countdown! Looks can be deceiving, though, for these primates have turned war into a fight for the whole family.

Wildlife educator Susan Kleven knows all about the lemur's secret weapon.

These lemurs are marching to battle, and it's women and children first. That's because in a lemur troop, it's the females that are large and in charge. So in a fight for their territory, the females (and their babies) are in the front line!

The main reason these animals are number four in the countdown is that when it comes to fighting, lemurs really stink. First of all, they mark their territory using special scent glands on their wrists. Lemurs also invented "stench warfare," as wildlife educator Susan Kleven explains:

Ring-tailed lemurs fight using a scent gland that's on their wrist. They rub it with their hands. They actually transfer the scent from the glands onto their hands and then on their tail. They fling scent at one another and this helps to establish territory. It's pretty stinky to a ring-tailed lemur.

Lemurs rub a supremely stinky scent onto their hands, then fling it at their opponents.

Male lemurs are extreme wimps. They're terrified of the females, and will only fight other males by flinging perfume at each other with their tails! It's an extremely safe way of fighting. And it's found its way into the research laboratories of the U.S. Department of Defense!

Scientists are hoping to design a smell so they can fight like a lemur. But nobody will wear this perfume on their wrist because researchers aim to invent the worst smell in the world.

Imagine if you could use smell as an offensive weapon. You could clear the streets in no time if you dropped the ultimate stink bomb. And unlike rubber bullets and tear gas, the only thing a stink bomb would hurt is your nose! It seems that bad smells are big news for more than just the lemur!

The
Tasmanian Devil

When traveling in Tasmania—never, ever pick a fight with the devil. The Tasmanian devil is number three in the countdown because it's such a ferocious fighter. Its life is a constant battle fought with jaws eight times more powerful than a Doberman's. They leave painful wounds that can sometimes be fatal.

The Tasmanian devil has to be ferocious to survive its harsh life.

Usually the only time devils meet is to fight for food or for mates. So for the Tasmanian devil, being aggressive is a good survival strategy. The better you fight, the better your chances of a mate and a meal.

Like Tasmanian devils, some fighters just love to dominate. It doesn't matter how hard they train or how strong they are—sometimes their aggressiveness comes from within. Aggression has been linked to hormones—especially the hormone testosterone.

These creatures have extremely high levels of testosterone, so they're always ready for a fight.

Scientists have found that when men are put in a confrontational situation, testosterone is released from the gonads and floods the bloodstream. Some studies have shown that the person with higher levels of testosterone will tend to be more aggressive and dominate the situation.

There may also be a link between our testosterone levels and the professions we choose. Actors have higher levels of testosterone than ministers. Working women have higher levels of testosterone than women who stay at home. And delinquents have higher levels of testosterone than college students.

For many men, just watching sports is enough to get the testosterone flowing. If you support the winner, you could have testosterone levels twice the normal levels! But back a loser and plummeting testosterone may mean you have a hard time growing a beard the next morning! Females also produce testosterone, but the hormone makes few females as aggressive as the she-devil. This female has decided that her mate's been mooching around her burrow for too long. It's time to take out the trash.

In this battle of the sexes, the female always wins. The male is back to roaming the forest alone, picking fights with other devils.

The only match for a male Tasmanian devil is a she-devil. Now that's fierce!

2 The Fighting Fish

To find number two in our countdown of extreme fighters in its homeland, you have to travel to Southeast Asia. Once these fighters were found in the shallow, dirty waters of irrigation ditches and rice paddies. That's because number two in the countdown is a fish.

At number two in our countdown, this "beautiful warrior" has a deadly side.

It doesn't look much like a fighter, but its scientific name—*Betta splendens*—translates as "beautiful warrior." Its good looks have made it a popular aquarium fish, but there's a problem.

These warriors need special care and attention because they're born to fight. They're so aggressive that they have to be kept in solitary confinement, according to Faith, a Los Angeles Betta breeder. She explains:

The main challenge that us Betta breeders have is that we have to deal with this aggressive behavior and isolate all of these fish. It causes us a lot of logistic problems—we have to have thousands of jars, each fish has to be in a separate jar, and if they did not have that aggressive behavior it would certainly make our hobby a lot easier and more enjoyable.

Fighting fish are so aggressive, each one has to have its own jar.

Bettas are number two in the countdown because if you put two males in the same tank, they'll use their razor-sharp teeth to rip each other to shreds. The loser can sometimes bleed to death. Faith explains:

We do not know why Bettas are so aggressive, but I have heard of an experiment where two males were taken to a lake and basically released into the center of the lake and they had the entire lake to themselves and they proceeded immediately to fight each other. So we conclude it's not a matter of territory or space because they had an entire lake and it was a new territory for them. It's a matter of alpha dominance. In each tank you'll have one fish, female or male, that would be the alpha fish. As long as you keep that one fish in there it will keep everyone in line. If you remove that fish, everyone else fights, so it suggests there's an alpha dominance that needs to be established.

If this male had to share a tank, it would try to rip its tank mate to shreds.

And it's this alpha dominance that gave these "beautiful warriors" another name. For these are the legendary Siamese fighting fish!

In Thailand "fish fighting" was once a popular sport. People placed bets on which warrior would survive the battle, just like in the Colosseum of ancient Rome. Like Siamese fighting fish, gladiators were trained to kill in the name of entertainment.

In Thailand, some people used to bet on which fish would win a fight.

Although their lives were often short and brutal, gladiators were the rock stars of their day. In Pompeii, someone scribbled a piece of graffiti on a wall that suggested that the gladiator Celadus was a heartthrob. One Roman senator's wife was even said to have preferred gladiators to her country, her children, and her husband! It just goes to show that both fighting men and fighting fish can win the hearts of the girls!

1 The **Ant**

In the frozen forests of northern Europe, the most extreme fighters on the planet sit in a fortress waiting for spring. Each giant mound is home to a million or more . . . ants.

These giant mounds in the frozen forests of northern Europe are home to the planet's ultimate warriors.

Ants are number one in the countdown because when ants go to war, nothing can stand in their way. Ants are the ultimate warriors because some individuals are literally born to fight. In addition to the ordinary worker ants, some colonies create a caste of professional fighters.

Some ant colonies have their very own cadre of professional fighters.

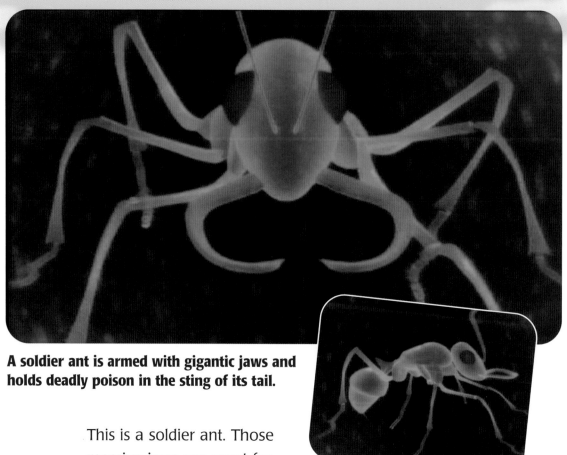

A soldier ant is armed with gigantic jaws and holds deadly poison in the sting of its tail.

This is a soldier ant. Those massive jaws are great for fighting, but not much else. It can't even feed itself and relies on other ants to bring it food to keep it fighting fit.

But these soldiers are also equipped with chemical weapons. A sting in the tail of the ant can inject a deadly poison. Individually each soldier is armed to the teeth, but what makes the ant army so deadly is the sheer weight of numbers. For when ants fight, it really is the attack of the clones.

Imagine if the U.S. Army were like an ant colony, and all the soldiers were sisters! In her lifetime, one ant queen could give birth to more soldiers than there are in the entire U.S. military!

This is the most extreme fighting force the world has ever seen. There can be up to 20 million sisters living in the biggest single colony of any animal on earth. For these are army ants.

These soldiers are such terrifying fighters that anything that gets in their way is in big trouble, according to Jane Stevens from the St. Louis Zoo. She explains:

Army ants are so vicious that they have even been known to attack humans.

> *Army ants are some of the most vicious animals on the planet. These animals are completely driven to get from point A to point B and will destroy anything in their path. They won't stop no matter what. They will go after tarantulas, and lizards and frogs and toads. They have even attacked humans from time to time.*

Ants are so aggressive that they even attack each other.

Ants also attack ants. They're so aggressive that scientist Edward Wilson once said, "If ants had nuclear weapons, they'd probably end the world in a week!"

Even without bombs, ant battles can be devastating. It begins when a scout sees an intruder from a neighboring colony. The alarm is raised, and reinforcements pour out of the nest. Ants are smart, though. They won't commit to a war unless they think they can win. So they calculate the other colony's strength by judging how many workers show up to battle. They recognize their sisters by odor, and separate immediately. Only if they sniff an advantage will they send in all available reinforcements to start fighting.

Just as in human wars, the worst defeats occur when one side has miscalculated the strength of the opposition. Tactical ant warfare has even attracted interest from human defense analysts. They're taking a close look at ants to try to sharpen their own techniques at estimating the strength of the enemy!

For the ants that get it wrong, the results are devastating. Their colony can be completely overwhelmed. The victorious colony will kill the queen, steal the food supplies, and even make slaves of the defeated workers. To try to prevent the devastation of their colony, one race of Asian ants has developed the ultimate warrior. This ant has a huge gland inside its abdomen. In extreme combat, it will rupture its own body wall, causing the gland to explode!

The ants are like walking grenades, spraying sticky toxic material all over the enemy! These extreme fighters make the ultimate sacrifice to protect their colony. That's why when it comes to fighting, the ant really is…The Most Extreme!

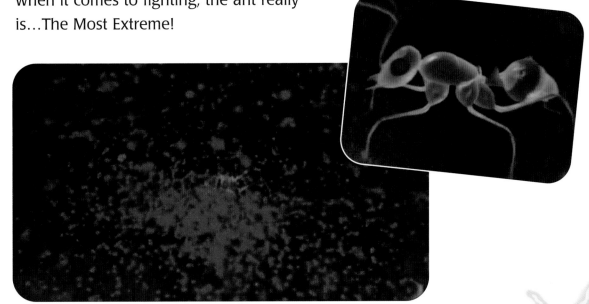

A type of Asian ant (above) will make its own body explode to spray toxic material (left) all over its enemy. Now that's extreme!

For More Information

Melissa Cole, *Lions.* San Diego: Blackbirch, 2002.

Eleanor J. Hall, *Polar Bears.* San Diego: KidHaven, 2002.

Elaine Landau, *Siamese Fighting Fish.* New York: Children's Press, 1999.

Katherine Lasky, *Shadows in the Dawn: The Lemurs of Madagascar.* San Diego: Harcourt Brace, 1998.

Elaine Pascoe, *Ants.* San Diego: Blackbirch, 1998.

Elaine Pascoe, *Mantids.* San Diego: Blackbirch, 2004.

April Pulley Sayre, *Army Ant Parade.* New York: Henry Holt, 2002.

Christy Steele, *Tasmanian Devils.* Chicago: Raintree, 2003.

Jason and Jody Stone, *Polar Bear.* San Diego: Blackbirch, 2001.

John Woodward, *Ants.* Danbury, CT: Grolier, 2001.

Glossary

brawn: muscular strength

callous: a thickened, enlarged area on the outer skin

concussion: brain injury

Doberman: breed of dog known for aggressiveness

dominance: great influence or control over others

gland: an organ that removes materials from the blood and secretes them for a different purpose.

gonad: sex gland

grenade: small bomb thrown by hand or shot from a launcher

logistical: relating to the management of an operation

moat: protective trench

rice paddy: wet land used for growing rice

solitary: without companions

tactical: having to do with military operations

toxic: capable of causing injury or death

Index